SUPERHEROES

BY MARK ROGERS

CURRENCY PRESS
The performing arts publisher

GRIFFIN
THEATRE
COMPANY

CURRENT THEATRE SERIES

First published in 2020
by Currency Press Pty Ltd,
PO Box 2287, Strawberry Hills, NSW, 2012, Australia
enquiries@currency.com.au
www.currency.com.au

in association with Griffin Theatre Company

Typeset by Dean Nottle for Currency Press.
Cover design by Alphabet.
Cover features Gemma Bird Matheson; photo by Brett Boardman.

Currency Press acknowledges the Traditional Owners of the Country on which
we live and work. We pay our respects to all Aboriginal and Torres Strait
Islander Elders, past and present.

A catalogue record for this
book is available from the
NATIONAL
LIBRARY
OF AUSTRALIA
National Library of Australia

Contents

For Ash, Edith and Sanja.

Superheroes was first produced by Griffin Theatre Company at the Reginald Theatre at the Seymour Centre, Sydney, on 25 September 2020, with the following cast:

EMILY	Gemma Bird Matheson
JANA	Claire Lovering
SIMON / DINO	Aleks Mikic

Director, Shari Sebbens
Dramaturg, Declan Greene
Designer, Renée Mulder
Lighting Designer, Verity Hampson
Composer and Sound Designer, David Bergman
Associate Composer and Sound Designer, Alyx Dennison
Stage Manager, Khym Scott

CHARACTERS

EMILY, 22
JANA, 30
SIMON / DINO, 23

SETTING

Sydney and then Thirroul, New South Wales, Australia.
Mostar, Bosnia-Herzegovina.

NOTES

A / indicates point of interruption.

A character dash — followed by no text, indicates an unspoken action, or the choice not to say anything.

An … at the end of a line means a trailing off, or an invitation for the other person to speak.

Words in brackets ( ) are unspoken, but the vibe of them should come across in a silence, or a voiced sound or even just a nod.

CAPITALS DON'T ALWAYS MEAN LOUDER.

No accents.

This play went to press before the end of rehearsals and may differ from the play as performed.

JANA ONE

It starts with a list of war crimes and goes swiftly downhill.

Forced removal of civilians.
Detention of civilians.
Starvation. Beatings. Torture.
The use of human shields.
Wanton destruction not justified by military necessity.
Bridges. Courts. Mosques blah blah blah.
The ethnic cleansing of Bosnian Muslims.
Thirty-two separate incidents.

Why do I smell popcorn? I can smell popcorn all of a sudden.

The courtroom is like a caricature of a courtroom. Wood panelling and grey carpet, a little desk mic for anyone who gets to speak. The little French judge wears a red coat that is straight out of *Star Trek*. His little goblin voice drones. Murder and sexual violence! At the box the General is standing tall. His beard groomed and white. A sheen of sweat on his forehead. It's warm at The Hague.

The list ends and the French judge coughs into a microphone.

The court dismisses the prosecution's appeal concerning Mr Praljak and affirms the sentence of twenty years of imprisonment. Guilty. Knew it. Mr Praljak, you may be seated.

But he doesn't. He doesn't sit. He's meant to sit but he doesn't. He—

Judges, it is with disgust that I reject this verdict.

Mr Praljak. Stop, please sit down. They're trying to move on but he won't let them. Slobodan Praljak is not a war criminal!

I hear the microwave in the kitchen ding and Mina walks into the room with a fresh bowl of popcorn. Baka turns on her, you should be watching, you should be watching this!

He says it again. Slobodan Praljak is not a war criminal! The camera snaps to a close-up. The General lifts something to his lips. A small glass, like a shot glass or— His hands barely shake as he tips the contents into his mouth. The camera pans away. I want them to cut back to the General, cut back to the General. He's shouting now, they've turned his microphone off. I can't hear what he's—

Then the interpreters repeat him in English.

Baka grabs my arm—what did they say? What did they say he said?

He said it was poison.

The four generations of my family crammed into our lounge room in West Mostar.

Sit in astonished silence.

Then there's an explosion of joy, they're screaming, pointing their fingers at the TV, my uncles are high-fiving, clapping, crying. Mina is outraged—you're all fucked, she's muttering into her popcorn, you're all crazy, he's just killed himself! Which is sort of how I feel too but Baka is laughing, actually laughing, smiling, hugging! Hugging. She never—Mina swears at us, you're fucking crazy and she's right I feel it, I feel crazy. But then my aunties start singing and I can't help it, I can't stop it, it's like we've just won the World Cup.

In my heart.

In my country's heart.

Pride.

EMILY ONE

I wake up early and walk into the backyard of my house. It's not light yet. The air is still and warm. When I reach the only place on the property that gets Vodafone reception, I see I have no new messages from Simon. And I just stand there. Not thinking. Not wondering. I'm quite blank. I'm still in my socks. The dew on the grass is soaking into them. I don't mind. It's lovely just standing there.

Then all of a sudden it starts like an ad before a YouTube clip.

Do it now. You have to do it now.

Now. Now. Now. Now. Now.

I try to keep it light. I kick things off with—'Hiya! Exclamation point!'—and use phrases like 'but no stress' and 'if you have time' and 'it's important that we clear the air given recent developments'. To strike the right tone I keep having to add things, qualifiers, double and even triple negatives. 'Not that I'm not saying that I don't want to be together lol.' The number of commas I am using per sentence is honestly offensive. The text message is an abomination. In real life I am not winking. I am not sticking my tongue out.

I hit send and throw my phone away into the grass.

I'm not gonna check it.

How do you not write back to that message?

I sit on the toilet and rub my housemate's Moroccan Oil through my split ends, pulling out knots. It hurts but that's helping. By using this am I directly contributing to deforestation in Brazil or is that only if I'm the one who buys it? Maybe he doesn't have credit. Maybe he's lost his phone. My hair feels fucking amazing. I scroll back up through our text chains. Five days ago he replied to my Instagram story with the one hundred emoji. He's only does this when I post my poems. Or when they have cleavage.

I stand up and look at myself in the mirror. I run the shower so the mirror fogs up and artfully arrange my top. Then I stick my neck forward and tilt my head and take about fifty photos until I can see that my face has the right combo of sad and hot and thoughtful. I have to walk back outside to post it with the caption: 'vibes'.

Some words have become stuck in my head. Bildungsroman. *Roman á clef*. Anti-novel. They ache. I don't know why.

Ba-doop. My phone.

I copy-paste the abomination and DM him.

Three dots appear then disappear.

If he leaves me on read I might run in front of traffic.

He doesn't. I should have guessed he'd gotten a new sim. He suggests we meet at the Courty. I do mental maths then casually propose we meet at Camperdown Park. I say more private but I mean that I'm broke. Dope. Less gronks lol hunnid. We're being brilliantly mature. I've told him. I've told him and for the first time in weeks it looks like everything might actually be going to be okay. Then I get a text from Mum.

Fuuck!

where are you? ewen's bday today. G not happy.

She's ended it with a smiley face.

I don't think she's smiling in real life.

JANA TWO

Baka stalks through the apartment. Where's your sister? Somewhere along the way my family designated me Mina's minder. I don't know, I say.

Mina's bedroom door creaks open. Baka is up before I can stop her. She catches her in the hallway, Beats by Dre on her ears and a bag slung over her shoulder. I'm meant to be going out. Too good for this family, are you? Today is important. Mina snaps back in the new voice she's been using since starting university—that man does not deserve to be celebrated. Those terrible things he did? Terrible things? Baka shrugs. He did nothing, nothing. Mina says, yeah stood by and did nothing while his men— Does he have eyes in the back of his head? Baka says. I say at least we can both agree that whatever he may have done, these are complex issues that— Mina starts laughing, who asked you here, the UN? Baka starts shouting, you think this is a joke? This is all funny to you? A man's died! Mina matches her, honestly Baka, didn't he deserve to? Okay, I put myself physically between them, let's all just calm down. Fine, Mina says, I'm going out anyway. For your new gypsy man, is it? Baka spits. Roma, Baka, it's 2017, we don't say gypsy, Mina launches into her usual speech about the new multi-ethnic, multicultural Bosnia. Baka regroups to the kitchen. Mina stares at me. She's insane, right? You weren't alive during the war, I say. Oh yeah, thanks, Mina grabs her bag and pushes her way past. I'm glad I wasn't, it made you both stupid. The front door of our apartment slams shut behind her.

I find Baka at the kitchen table. She's like a statue. The tyrant who brought us up, absently eating handfuls of cold popcorn. Mina's crazy for trying to change her, she's eternal.

Let's make something for everyone tonight, I say. I'll shop. Baka looks up. She waves her hand, we can just order something. No, I say, today is important. Baka smiles for the second time, a personal record, and begins outlining a meticulously detailed list of the many, many things she'll need from several specific locations all across the city. The place with the grapes out front she says, not the place near the entrance. And don't bring me any of that halal shit, okay?

Of course Baka, whatever you want.

EMILY TWO

Cross-cultural innovations and feminist coming-of-age narratives in contemporary Australian literature. Three thousand words. Due midnight. I haven't done the readings. I email the tutor a frantic sob story—ANXIETY AND END OF SESSION RELATED TRAUMA— and request an extension while I'm sitting in the car out the front of Mum's place.

No present for Ewen. How old is he, even? Three? Six? I search the weirdly gritty? mess of clothes and garbage in the backseat and find a tote bag from the MCA. I don't have anything to wrap it in. There's a random roll of toilet paper, which I do consider seriously for a bit.

The doorbell sings and I see Gemma walk up the corridor through the mesh. From the way she flicks the flyscreen unlocked I know that 'not happy' doesn't cover it. CLLIIICCCK. Sorry I'm late. She doesn't say anything. Just turns and yells—Aunty Em's here! Ewen barrels into my legs wearing a full Spiderman costume, mask and all, speaking too fast for me to pick out individual syllables. He made us wait till you were here to do the cake, Gemma says, most of the kids have gone home. I pick him up. Happy birthday, bud! Mum limps into view down the end of the corridor on her crutches, and immediately deploys her most effective weapon. Disappointment. Hi, sweetie, you made it! Ewen, insane from the five seconds where he wasn't the centre of attention, whacks the side of my head. AUNTY PRESENT!

Okay! Are you ready? Happy birthday! It's a tote bag! Yeah! It's really cool! It's from Sydney! Yeah! Hey but the real present, the real present is a day out at the museum with me! It's an IOU! Do you know what an IOU is, mate?! It means I OWE YOU a trip to the Museum of Contemporary Art! You'll love it! The art is so amazing! So great for kids! In the meantime maybe you can keep your toys in it!

Ewen hands the bag to his mum and runs off, unmoved.

Such a thoughtful gift! chirps Mum. Gemma doesn't say anything.

Didn't Matt come? I press one of Gemma's reliable bruises. Dodged out when I wanted cash for the cake, she says. Mum adds—but at least Ewie loves his costume! Second-hand, Gemma says. Didn't even wash it.

They're both as bad as each other. Wollongong's two biggest martyrs living together. Two thirds of my AusStudy for a literal rat's nest in Tempe but god, it's worth it.

My phone vibrates. Not Simon. Email from my tutor—surprised, Emily, not like you, doctor's certificate needed, apply for academic consideration through student central blah blah—arsehole, you're teaching a course on feminist narrative, the women in the class should get nineteen per cent extra time for submission to compensate for the pay gap.

Ewen's pulling me by the hand. I can't, mate, I have an assignment due.

Are you serious? Gemma says. You couldn't have finished it before you came?

I've had stuff on.

He's your nephew, she says, like that's some kind of ultimatum. She kneels down and uses the talking-to-baby voice I hate.

What did you want to show Aunty, Ewie?

MOVIE! he yells, shooting imaginary webs from his wrists.

He's been saving it, she says. He's waited all day.

After my assignment, I say. Once I finish we can watch it together, okay, bud?

Gemma's face withers me.

I promise.

JANA THREE

It is stunning outside. The air is sweet with paprika. I smoke a cigarette as I walk down Fra Ambre Miletića towards the markets on the other side of the river. A kid runs past me wearing the Croatian flag as a cape. More flags are being hung out the windows of apartment blocks. The churches ring the bells for mass.

Today, Mostar is the most beautiful city on earth.

I pass a line of cops at the old bridge, the scene of the General's supposed crime. Oblivious tourists stop to snap photos. One of the cops lets me pass. How come the vegetables on their side are always better? I laugh. It's a mystery.

I buy much more than even Baka said we needed. The image of my whole family around a table, stuffing themselves on olives, sarma, dolma, pilaf, ćevapi, tomatoes and fried okra. It's too intoxicating. I buy bags of stuff. Too many bags. They cut white lines into my fingers but I don't care, I want everything.

At the highway crossing on the way home, my arms ache. I want to put the bags down but I have to rush across at the first gap in traffic. Hundreds of cars speed past on their way north to Sarajevo or south to Dubrovnik. Bosnia's elegant cities. Ow. There's always one shitty bag, I think, when—

The sound tears through my skull like shock. Like the memory of pain.

Gunshots.

Gunshots. Fuck.

Fuck.

Oh, fuck.

EMILY THREE

What does any of this have to do with anything? I'm putting all my quotes in order in the hope it makes an argument appear but the ideas are all disconnected. There's no discernable through-line or relationship between them. They're just words hanging in white space.

I can't focus. Mum's hobbling around cleaning things that are, to the untrained eye, very clean already and Gemma is having a lie-down so no-one's watching Ewen. He keeps snatching the headphones off my ears.

Are you in great distress or grave danger? he says, too close to my face. No, mate, just trying to pass university. And I put my headphones back on.

I'll save you! he screams, ripping them off again.

I'm afraid I'm okay, Spiderman. I don't really need saving right now.

Yes you do, he says. You're the girl.

Sometimes you can just tell who this kid's dad is. He starts shouting. You're the girl. You're the girl!

Okay, I know you're just a kid but girls don't always have to be the ones getting saved, okay? That is like, actually a pretty mean thing to think. Do you see how that makes it seem like girls are weaker than boys? We're not, actually, see? I push him down on the couch and hold him there while he squirms. He's laughing. You can't get up, can you? And who's going to save you? The laugh becomes a yell. I press harder. See? Boys don't have to always be the ones who leap to the rescue. He's crying now but for the sake of his future relationships with women I think it's still worth emphasising that—That. Attitude. Is. Not. Very. Nice. For. The. Girls.

Gemma bolts into the room and tears me off him. He's bawling.

We were playing, I say.

Gemma is spectacular with rage. What the fuck are you doing?

Ewen has snot streaming from his nose. Hey hey sorry, mate, so sorry, hey shh shh shh shh shhh, hey how about we watch the movie, hey? Let's watch the movie now, what do you reckon, Spiderman, should we watch your movie?

The sniffles don't stop until Gemma jams the DVD into the slot. A delicate silence takes hold of the lounge room. Gemma breathes out really slowly, something Mum used to do when we drew on the wall of our latest rental.

The stupid Marvel flipbook credit sequence starts up.

My phone buzzes. Simon's new number. Gemma is staring at me. I can't answer.

Today is bullshit.

JANA FOUR

They're firing into the air. Uniformed police have pulled over a van onto the shoulder of the highway. I can't see who's in it. The police yell for them to get out. A man does. Dark, with a close-cropped beard. He puts his hands above his head, they aren't even pointing their guns at him. They yell for his licence. His papers. He starts speaking his language, talking really fast. A woman gets out of the car too. She's wearing a scarf on her head like some of the Bosniak women do, but she's too dark to be Bosniak.

She's saying English? English? The police are shaking their heads. They ask again for their papers.

The woman doesn't understand. She's looking around, desperate.

She yells out to me, do you speak English?

I look away but she can tell I understood.

Please, she shouts, can you speak for us? You can speak with them. She starts walking towards me.

The police put their guns up but she keeps walking. They're aiming this way, at me at, don't bring me into—

You speak English.

I mumble, sorry. I don't really have time. She doesn't listen.

Tell them. We have papers.

One of the cops comes over and asks me what I'm doing.

I speak to him in Croatian, they say they have papers.

Papers, she repeats in English. Documents from your government.

The cop gestures for her to hand them over then squints at the print. He speaks into the radio clipped to the front of his body armour.

Please, you will help us. We are refugees. Her English is terrible. Rote phrases learnt out of some guidebook. It's hardly skilled migration.

The cop signs off on his radio and after a little moment of pretending to look again at the papers, he throws them to the wind, scattering them into the air where they're caught in the slipstream of a truck and whirled across the tarmac.

The woman screams.

I shouldn't be here. I don't want to see this.

She starts speaking to me really fast. Her face looms in front of mine. This is nothing to do with me, I say, but she's still talking, too quick for me to understand— Then one of the car doors swings open. The police start yelling. They rush at the man, knocking him to the ground, they put his head against the road.

But running towards the woman, from the car, there's a small boy. A little younger than my nephews. Dark eyes. He's crying. He grabs at his mother's skirt and she lifts him up. Still looking at me she says it again.

We are refugees blah blah blah blah blah.

Speak slower, I can't understand what you're saying.

Tell them we do not want to stay in your stupid country. She turns to scream at the cops, we are trying to get to Europe!

Fuck this. Fucking disrespect. I start walking away, further up the highway to find somewhere else to cross. She chases after and grabs my arm, please, she's saying. Let go of me. She's squeezing hard enough to bruise. OW. She's babbling, garbled English stuck on repeat. You can speak for us, please, you can help. She holds tight. Please, she says, please, please help and it's quite weird because somewhere deep inside my head there's this noise that goes:

I DON'T CARE I DON'T FUCKING CARE I HAVE THINGS TO PLACES TO I DON'T HAVE TIME TO FUCKING AND IT'S NOT MY FAULT YOUR COUNTRY IS YOU CAN'T BLAME ME DON'T BLAME ME WHEN IT'S NOT MY AND I CAN'T HELP HOW AM I MEANT TO HELP WHAT GOOD WOULD SO I CAN'T WON'T

CAN'T ANYWAY I'M BUSY ANYWAY I DON'T HAVE ROOM
I'M FULL JUST LEAVE ME LEAVE ME THE FUCK ALONE
BECAUSE HONESTLY HONESTLY I DON'T GIVE A SHIT A
FUCKING SHIT ABOUT YOU AND YOUR PLEASE PLEASE
PLEASE PLEASE PLEASE YOU CAN FUCKING **DIE** YOU CAN
FUCKING **DIE** FOR ALL I FUCKING FUCK OFF NOW JUST
FUCK OFF BACK WHEREVER YOU WHEREVER THE FUCK
NOT HERE PLACE YOU FUCKING AND STOP **GRABBING** AT
ME **STOP GRABBING AT ME** STOP FUCKING GRABBING AT
ME I DON'T HAVE ROOM IN MY HEART TO CARE

and I take a ripe tomato from my shopping bag and hurl it at her. I
expect it to miss but it doesn't. It explodes on the centre of her chest. I
throw another and it hits her legs. She turns away but I keep going. The
next hits the back of her head. The police are looking and laughing,
they pick up the bearded man and point to what I'm doing. I throw
another—it splits when it hits her. Red fruit stains her headscarf.
Everything my Baka went through. Her rages. The way she still walks
in zigzags. The fear and the hunger and Mum's lungs near the end,
caked with the dust of a city shelled to the edge of madness. For this?
She's on the ground, crawling. I throw one dead on; it hits her kidneys
with a satisfying thud. That'll bruise, I think. That'll leave a fucking
mark.

I send a prayer of silent thanks to Slobodan Praljak.

Then the boy sobs, exposed now the woman's fallen. It's probably not
even her child, just a prop.

I reach back into the bag and take aim.

The tomatoes smell as rich as summer fields.

And then I see it happen. I see it happen before it actually happens. It
hangs in my imagination like a mirage. Or a stone.

The boy runs from the woman, but blindly, in panic. Just to get away,
just as an expression of terror. He runs away from me and the woman
in the scarf, away from the police, away from the man on the ground
next to the car. In the only direction he can run.

Onto the highway.

Onto the highway and he—

A car.

A Skoda.

White.

A white Skoda.

The word I'm thinking is flattens. It flattens him.

He doesn't fly into the air.

He's too little.

So it just—

Knocks him into the ground.

And the car keeps going.

Keeps driving.

And the woman must really be the child's mother because the sound that comes from her is wrenching.

It lacerates.

It burns out of her body and is immediately swallowed up by the sound of cars and trucks driving down the M6.1 past the university on the way north to Sarajevo.

EMILY FOUR

I would fuck Chris Hemsworth in a heartbeat but this movie sucks. It's so stupid. Like, why is it that while all the Avengers are flying around and blowing shit up you never see the ordinary people? Like, ah man, can't go to work today because some alien threw the Hulk into my building. They're meant to be saving humanity and they never even seem to SEE any of the humans they're doing it for. And like, is there still a government in this reality? Or is the fate of the whole world decided by magical rich people with superpowers? How can one person even BE responsible for that? The arrogance of it is unbelievable. And the stakes, man, the stakes are so fucking big everything's meaningless. And the hard decisions are all like, I can save all life in the universe, or my one true love—and in the end they get to save both! You don't get both! You have to pick. And if that choice ends up defining you then suck shit, Captain America, that's that. Should have done something else. Saved no-one. Gone to the shops. These fucking movies. This fucking lie that everything's going to be alright.

Fourth missed call from Simon. He must finally get that I can't answer because he texts. I have to pretend I have to go to the toilet to check it. Gemma is all over me.

I look at myself in the bathroom cabinet mirror. I look fucking awful.

How long's it take to piss? Gemma yells from the lounge room. I can hear Ewen's voice sliding up the octave. Movie. Movie! MOVIE!

I sneak out the back door without saying goodbye.

I drive to the beach near Mum's.

I send Simon a dropped pin then sit, looking out at the grey sky, the black ocean and the lights of the shipping tankers sitting on the border between them.

Sometimes—but only sometimes because mostly it's shit—Thirroul is the most beautiful place on earth.

— Hey.

— Heya.

— Hi.

  They hug.

  It's nice here.

— Yeah it is.

— Nowhere to get a coffee though, I was fanging for a coffee. A coffee or a beer. So I got a sixpack cos they were open, but I guess now I just have this sixpack all to myself which is a bit of a sad vibe.

— Go for it.

— By myself?

— If you want one.

— I sort of do but is it a weird vibe? Like does it make me seem a bit like a homeless person.

— It's fine.

— Cheers then

He cracks the beer. Sips.

— Did you do anything last night?

— Yeah, nothing much hey.

— Did you do something?

— Um, yeah. Not really—

— Who with?

— What?

— Who did you not really do this something with? Where was it?

— Um

— Where were you?

— I don't know.

— You don't know?

— I dunno, yeah, around.

— That's very strange that you don't know.

— I was at a party.

— That's right! For at least some of last night you were at Craig from uni's party because I saw his Instagram story and you were playing ping-pong. And weirdly enough so was Sarah because her story last night also included a ping-pong table and a bonfire and she tagged Craig in it and wrote best party evah with a h on the end.

— You follow Sarah?

— Yes.

— She let you?

— I made one as a Sydney Actors' Agency and added her.

— Fuck, man.

— Are we together or are we not together because I'm confused.

— I left when she got there.

— How am I meant to believe that?

— To be clear we weren't, I mean, we weren't together when I was with Sarah. You and me, we were never together together.

— What were we then?

— I don't know, we were just hanging out. Is this really what we're / going to talk about?

— You don't cum in someone who you're just fucking. You do that with your girlfriend. You do that with the person you're together together with.

— You said you were on the pill.

— Not my point.

— I don't know how you remember it but we were both a bit caught up / at that particular moment.

— There is no qualification you can make here, Simon. It's not the kind of thing people who are 'just hanging out' do with each other.

— No, but—

— So you can see why I'm confused.

— I can see that, yeah

— You can see why you being at that party, whether you 'left when she got there' or not, is contributing to my sense of confusion.

— Nothing happened.

— Okay.

— I would tell you if it did. It didn't.

—

— And you're right, I have not been clear with you.

— Yeah.

— You're right.

— I know I'm right. I'm telling you I am.

— Sorry yes, of course you are, I know, I'm

—

— I'm sorry.

—

— I really am.

—

— Nothing is going on with me and Sarah. I promise.

— Okay.

— I like having sex with you way more anyway.

> *They watch the waves.*

Actually, I have something I want to—okay and this is, like, a bit weird or whatever but I wanted to read you this letter, it's not, I was gunna send it as a message but then that seemed a bit throwaway so I wrote it down but then, you know, obviously I should probably do it to your face but if I just tried to wing it, like make it up on the spot, it would be shit and not say what I mean so I've written down what I want to say. I know it's a bit—anyway—I'm nervous now—anyway I'm just going to start.

> *He gets out a folded-up piece of paper and opens it. It's a bit too dark to read it so he gets his phone light out and holds it up to the paper. He reads.*

Emily.

I know I haven't been the greatest guy to you. I have acted selfishly and boorishly. I have lied to you and broken my word. You probably think I'm a fuckhead. And I am. I hurt you and I am sorry. I have been a total fuckhead and I take responsibility for that.

I also want to say that I think you are the coolest chick in the world. You are astonishingly beautiful and alluring. You are smart. You are brave. You are kind. You are a unicorn and you deserve to be treated like one. I haven't done that. But I want to. I so so so so want to.

Alain Badiou says that love is the first radical step against a consumerist society that privileges the individual. To stand together and see the world from the perspective of the two, not the one, is revolutionary and transgressive and necessary.

Emily, I think we should have this baby together. I want to see the world from the perspective of the three of us. You will make an incredible mum. I want us to be a family.

I love you.

I know I've said that before but not acted like it. But I do.

I will support you. I will barrack for you. I will hold your hand.

Please keep it.

Simon.

I don't know why I said Simon because obviously it's from me I'm right here.

— Simon, I'm going to have a termination.

—

—

— Okay.

—

— Yeah.

—

— That's—

—

— Have you thought about this?

— Have I thought about it?

— Because—

— Have I thought about it? Yes, I've thought about it.

— No, yeah, obviously I know you've thought about it.

— I haven't been able to think about anything else.

— I just mean are you sure, are you a hundred per cent sure that's what you—?

— Yes. I mean a hundred percent, no, but—

— Ninety?

— I haven't thought about it in fucking number terms, Simon, I'm not a mathematician.

— But you're not totally sure, is what you're saying.

— Of course I'm not, I'm indecision personified. I have never in my life been totally sure about anything.

— Okay. So, I am about this. One hundred per cent.

—

— Genuinely.

— Fuck, Simon.

— I am.

— It's just—

— We can do it. I really really believe that we can. And it'll be hard. So hard but I I I dunno I just I really want to be hopeful about it and to to try because I love you and and and I know it's your decision but I'm asking you to please don't, please don't.

— I'm past nine weeks. I can't just take the pill or whatever.

— (oh jesus)

— I have to get a surgical now, where they like, scrape.

— (oh my god)

— It's five hundred bucks.

　　　　SIMON *shakes his head. They watch the waves.*

— There's this guy at work who always talks about his daughter. I used to think it was sort of pathetic, like he's working in a cinema still, he's not the manager and he's got this kid. But I don't know.

—

— Her name's Hermia

—

— He's so stoked on her, like, he'd say stuff about her all the time, he'd say. I love her more than anything, more than myself.

—

— I think I could be a great dad.

— Simon.

— I could. I would be great.

— It's not—

— I will love that kid. Our kid.

— It's not about that.

— You don't want to try? We could just try. I love you.

— You said.

— Even if you don't want to I dunno be with me. If you want to do it and I help or or we don't have to be together together but—

— So I bring it up myself and you pop over on weekends with a procession of new girlfriends.

— I won't have girlfriends.

— Sure.

— I won't. I will do whatever I need to make it work.

— If you want it so much why don't you take it?

— Hmm?

— Really it should be you who get first dibs, right?

— What?

— You should get the option to be the sole carer.

— That's—

— I'm serious. You're nice. You like writing and The Strokes. Your family is pretty well-off. If I was looking for someone to adopt to you'd be pretty high on the list.

— My family is not that well-off.

— You're its dad so if you want we don't even have to go through the courts. I just have the baby and then it goes and lives with you.

— By myself.

— Yeah.

— I—Yeah, I mean, yeah, that's something we could—

— If you want to be a father, I mean, this is like THE way to do it.

— Maybe.

— Maybe?

— Yeah, I mean it's something we could think about, isn't it?

— Why do you have to think about it?

— What?

— Why do you have to think about it? I don't have to think about it. If you want to take it you can. That's / easy for me.

— No, I mean that it's a big decision and—

— You said you wanted to be a part of its life.

— I do.

— So then—

— But it's different, isn't it? Doing it, I mean, would you actually want to give it up?

— I've just said that I would—yes—want that.

— Sure, but I mean, it's different. Saying it compared to—

— I absolutely mean it. What I say I mean. Do you want to take it, because—

— And and then, I mean it can live with me if you think—you could come and live with me too even—

— No. It lives with you, that's it. It doesn't see me.

— It doesn't see you.

— Yeah.

— Could you do that?

— I'm telling you I absolutely can.

— Sure but, in real life.

— This is real life.

— I know this is real life but we're just talking.

— You've noticed.

— Hypothetically. We're talking hypothetically—

— I'm not.

— In an ideal world—

— I'm not hypothesising.

— In an ideal world, we'd both want to be involved. Yes?

— No. I don't want to be involved.

— Well, you are involved.

— I'm not going to be its mother.

— How can you say that?

— How?

— You are its—you fucking are its mother you're going to push it out of your vagina, you're its mum.

— It was your sprog up inside me. Without the sprog there'd be nothing for me to push out, who's ultimately responsible here?

— You're growing it inside your body.

— If you're a gardener, and you plant a little onion plant, and it grows up and produces a big fucking onion, the biggest onion in the world, it wins prizes it's so big … do you say oh no it wasn't me, the soil is the real winner.

— I can imagine a scenario where some old dude would say that. Yes.

— For fuck's sake.

— What? I can.

— You have avoided the underlying principle of my metaphor.

— Well then your metaphor's shit, isn't it.

— Do you want to have the kid?

— I want us to have it.

— Why not just you?

— I want it to be us.

— Why do you want that?

— I said— / I love you, Emily.

— No. No. I'm asking a much more specific question. Why, for you, does it have to be us, in order to raise the baby, why does it have to be us?

— A kid needs a mum.

— Homophobic.

— It's not, no it's—

— Kids with two dads: not real kids according to you.

— No but one of them is the, you know, one's the mum figure, isn't it?

— I think you'll find they're both dad figures.

— Okay.

— I think you'll find that there's no such thing as innate female or male roles, mate, did you not attend Julia's fucking lectures?!

— No-one's a better ally to our gender-queer brothers and sisters than me.

— Why can't it be just you?

— I—fuck, jesus, I dunno. I dunno.

— Try to know. Please just try to make me understand.

— I mean where would I live? How would I, what would I feed it? Isn't formula like really bad for—and how would I pay for everything? I'd have to work. I'd have to quit the course for sure. I'd have to like like move out of my place probably and back in with my, it's not, it's not really an option for me right now.

— (oh, okay)

— I know that's probably exactly what you're—but it's not—

— You'd have to quit the course.

— No but in my head there's this this future, okay?

— You'd have to get a job.

— We live down here in some tree-house place in Coalcliff or Stanwell Park, and and we watch it crawl around our backyard.

— You'd have to move in with your parents? Jeez.

— And and, listen, I'm cooking spag bol and sneaking extra veggies into it while you two play on the living room carpet and we're listening to 'Blonde on Blonde' on vinyl

— Fuck, Simon.

— and we take turns putting her down to sleep and we read to her and we we we make sure you still have time to write and we get one of those cool-looking cloth things that you wear to put her in and we make up insane games and build cubbies and we're happy. We're happy. That's all I want. Isn't that what you want?

— Yes but—

— Isn't that way better?

— I don't know if it is

— It will be.

— I don't know that.

— Doing it, the two of us. Not even the two. The three. Together

— This is just words.

— Everything's words. Did you not attend Julia's lectures? Come on. It'll be you, me and her.

— Her.

— Yeah.

— You've decided, have you?

— No, but—

— You'd want a girl.

— It's just what I imagined.

— You're used to imagining girls I guess.

— Do you know already or—

— That's later.

— What do you think it is?

— You're not going to make me indulge in / thinking about it as some—

— Come on, what would you want it to be?

—

— Hypothetically.

—

— You must have thought about it.

— A girl.

— Knew it.

— World doesn't need more boys.

— Not like me anyway.

— No. Certainly not like you.

— I'm not so bad, though.

— Hmm.

— I'm pretty nice actually.

— You're a fuckhead.

— Yep. Totally I am. But I'm alright really.

— You're alright for a fuckhead.

— Yeah.

— Yeah.

—

—

— A baby girl.

They watch the waves. They turn to each other at the same time.

— Would it really be like that?

— Yes.

— Taking turns and time to write?

— Yes.

— Genuinely?

— We'd make it like that.

— And if it doesn't sleep and just screams all day you'll take it?

— Yes.

— And if I don't want to breastfeed?

— Fine.

— And when I can't have sex for months?

— Yeah, whatever.

They launch at each other. Kissing each other's faces madly. After a while it softens into a long hug. They stay like that, clinging to each other.
Then ...

— Are we really going to do this?

— Yes.

— This is insane.

— I know.

— I love you.

— I love you too.

They separate.

— So you'll have to get a job.

— Yeah! I mean I have a job.

— Two shifts a week at the Dendy.

— Once I finish honours I'll probably be tutoring so—

— Honours.

— Yeah.

— You're doing honours?

— Yeah, I thought we both would.

— Who's looking after it when we're at class or doing assignments?

— I don't know, your mum or my mum or—

— And if they have to work?

— We can get childcare.

— On two shifts a week at the cinema?

— We'll figure it out.

— We'll figure it out?

— We will. We are educated, resourceful, empathetic people, who, right now, are the exact kind of people who should be having kids.

— What if we break up?

— We won't.

— What if we do though?

— We won't.

— It's a statistical probability that we will.

— In the unlikely event that we break up I trust that we'd be able to act like responsible, fair-minded adults.

— Would you want full custody?

— We'd do fifty-fifty.

— And if I don't want that?

— We'd probably be one of those really chill divorced couples who know each other's lovers and have regular barbeques.

—

— What?

— It's just, what divorced couples have you been around?

— I don't know. Dan from work's divorced.

— Hermia's dad?

— Yeah but he sees her heaps, like every few weekends. And he's a chiller. He plays in this band. He's sort of an amazing tragic figure. I'm going to use him for a story I think.

> EMILY *gets up.*

Em?

— Oh my god.

— What?

— Fuck.

— What?

— hahahahahahhahaa

— Emily.

— Oh my god this is so pathetic.

— What is?

> SIMON *gets up.*

— I'm like, oh my god he wants the baby, he wants it with me, this guy is amazing, he's taking it seriously and he's going to help and I'm lapping it up, I'm lapping it up, even though my dad drives fucking taxis in Mackay and hasn't paid child support in like two decades, I'm like, yes, I'm going to raise a kid with this guy who doesn't even answer my texts.

— I got a new sim.

— You know why you want this baby, Simon? It's not because you love me. It's not because you think you'll make a great dad. It's not even because of what Alain Badiou says about transgressive togetherness or whatever. It's because, deep deep down, you think it will make you cool.

SIMON *starts shaking his head.*

— Oh, man, I really felt like I was going to slap you then.

SIMON *screams.*

AHHHHHHHHHHHHHHHHHHHHHHHHH!

— Don't yell.

— I dunno. No. It's fucked. It's fucked.

— What's fucked about it?

— It's just fucked.

— I can't do anything with that. Define what you mean by fucked.

— This whole thing is built on just some some assumption about what the future is going to be / and you're completely ignoring—

— Fuck off, we're not in a tutorial, Simon. Don't try and—

— Can I finish?

— Hahahahahahaha / oh my GODDD. You are such a dude.

— You're completely ignoring how I'm feeling.

— You think this isn't hard for me?

— I've actually had enough of your cross-examination thanks.

— This is smashing my heart in a million pieces.

— I just feel like you're—

— This is smashing my heart in a million pieces and I'M STILL DOING IT.

— You're so melodramatic.

— It may surprise you to hear this, but I too have / an idea of what my life is going to be like.

— This is classic, this is in your writing too, you know. The grand gesture. / The sacrifice.

— Fuck, you always know what to say.

— Yeah?

— You always know how to make me feel small.

— Because you are. Because it's true. Because you're a petty, tiny girl who doesn't know what she's doing.

— And you're a cunt.

— Fuck this.

>SIMON *starts to walk out.*

— Simon.

>*He stops, turns.*

>Can you please transfer me the money?

>SIMON *stares at* EMILY.

>I don't have enough money to pay for it myself.

>*He lifts up his hand and points at her. He points at her and doesn't say anything. He holds the point for ages. He might laugh. Then he shakes his head and drops his hand.*

— Good luck with it.

>*He walks away, up the beach, his feet sinking into sand.*
>EMILY *is alone.*
>*She looks up.*

— The sky is so big

JANA FIVE

Someone else is wearing me like a suit.

The officer hands me back my ID. It's no-one's fault, he says. It's no one here's fault. He believes it. I can see he does. Ha ha. Do I?

I move towards him. He takes a little step back and his eyes dart around. He's not sure what I'm doing. I'm not sure what I'm doing. I reach my arms out and wrap them around him. It's a hug, I think. I'm hugging this police officer. Why am I doing this?

Can I hold your gun?

He extricates himself from my grip and gently tells me to go home.

Please?

By the time I leave the police station it's dusk. The sky is rippled grey and orange. I have twenty missed calls from Baka. These stupid bags. Already rotting vegetables and souring milk. What? I only realise I'm calling Mina when I hear her voice. Hi. What did you do? Do? I— Baka's texting me, where are you? I don't know, there's a garbage bin, I'm outside, I'm— Call her, I'm busy, she's saying, I think, I'm not listening. A rat skitters along the gutter and buries itself in the overflowing filth on the footpath near the bin. Do you think I'm bad? Mina? She's hung up. I feel sick. The stink. Garbage. These bags. Rats.

I throw up next to the bin. It flops out of me like mince.

A bus pulls up down the road. Yes. Home.

EMILY FIVE

Simon's left his beers behind. Sand is stuck to the condensation on the bottles. More than anything else in the world I would like to drink one.

I don't. I watch the waves and the sky. There's no grey anymore. Just borderless black. The stars are stranded in the sky like passengers overboard some enormous fucking—fucking some ship or some shit. Who cares? Who cares about fucking poetry? Words don't do anything. They're just nothing, just air.

Who cares? Who cares? Who cares who cares who cares? Who fucking cares?

W h o c a r e s ?

Do you think I should walk into the sea?

JANA SIX

There are no seats on the number two bus to Rodoc Kampus. Just rows of heads looking at their phones and pretending not to see me. My feet ache. My arms feel like meat.

God.

I just want to put my bags down.

But the floor has that wet, slicked look. The line past the university always smells like piss. A beer bottle dislodges and rolls along the ground as we pull out of the station.

I see a boy, young man, sitting near me on a bench seat. Dark eyes. Skinny as nails in the Adidas tracksuit uniform of brain-dead youth world over. Could be Bosniak. Roma even.

What's he doing this side of the river? Today? Something could happen. He takes a swig from his Red Bull can. Idiot. Sitting there. Whose fault would it be, the boy, if something happened to him? Shouldn't even be here. Who's ultimately responsible? When it comes down to it, ultimately, who is to blame?

The answer swells in me like a bag of popcorn.

They are.

The whole fucking lot of them.

Taking up room.

Taking up space.

The fucking Afghans who came here.

Before them the fucking Turks.

The fucking Jews before them.

The fucking Serbs.

The fucking Slavs.

The fucking Austrians.

The fucking Macedonians.

The fucking Arabs.

The fucking Ottomans before all them, more fucking Turks with their fucking Islam.

And before them the Byzantines.

The Ostrogoths before that.

The Huns before them.

The Romans before that.

The fucking Greeks before them.

The Illyrian tribes. Bashing the shit out of each other.

The Danilo, with their fucking four-legged ceramic pots.

Then what?

The fucking Narva who killed the Kunda.

The fucking Kunda who killed the Swiderians.

The fucking Swiderians who came from nowhere with flint blades.

And just twenty-five miles from here. Before everything. Whoever made the carving at the Badanj Cave. A stick-figure horse with lines sticking out of its flank.

Arrows. Hundreds of them.

There's a metaphor for Europe if you ever wanted one. A horse pin-cushioned with arrows.

It's impossible to live here. If it's not rats it's mortar rounds. If it's not mortar rounds it's arrows.

Or tomatoes.

— Can you move?

— Sorry?

— Can you get up please, I need that seat.

— Pardon?

— I need that seat.

— The seat?

— Yes.

— What about it?

— Can you stand up and get out of it?

— Why?

— The bus is full. I need to sit.

— It's not reserved seating, is it?

— No.

— You don't have some special claim on it?

— No but—

— So you just want me to give up my seat?

— That's what I'm saying.

— Okay. Um. No. No way.

— Just get up.

— No.

— I really need to sit down.

— Bad luck.

— Okay. Please. Please can I have that seat you are sitting on?

— Ask someone else.

— I'm asking you.

— So just ask someone else then.

— Why not?

— Exactly, go ask them.

— No, why not you, why won't you stand up? What's the big deal?

— Is anyone hearing this?

— Yes yes, hi hi hi, everyone.

— You start talking to me out of nowhere.

— So?

— You're rude. You're really rude and then—

— I'm sorry for being rude, can I have the seat now?

— No. Because you're rude, you don't give me a good reason why you should get the seat, I've been at work all day, I got here early, I sat down, you accost me.

— I didn't / accost you.

— You accost me, yes you did and you don't say why I should give you my seat.

— I'm tired.

— So am I.

— My feet hurt and I want to put my bags down.

— Then put them down, jesus.

— On the floor?

— Yes, Christ. Why do you need—?

— ON THE PISS-COVERED FLOOR.

— Stop yelling.

— STOP SITTING IN MY SEAT.

— Okay, I don't really want to be a part of your public meltdown.

— What would it take?

— What?

— What do I have to do to get that seat?

— I dunno, you could try asking me nicely?

— Okay, fine. I am going to ask you nicely now. Very sweetly and meekly so you can feel like a big strong generous man when you give up your seat for the helpless little lady—

— Right okay, just fuck off now, alright?

— What's your name?

— What?

— I'm asking your name.

— What, are you going to report me?

— No.

— Who are you going to report me to? The fucking, / fucking, fucking—

— Okay, look—

— Bus police? Or something?

— I'm trying to take this down a notch.

— Fuck this. Take the seat. Fine. Take it. What do I care? Psycho.

— Excuse me?

— This is my stop anyway so—I said it's all yours you utter fucking pyscho.

— This is your stop? This next one.

— Yeah so, 'bye. 'Bye now, you fucking crazy person.

— You're getting off here, are you? Now?

— Yes, thank god. And thank all you for saying nothing! Thanks so much, guys. Bus driver, too. Good job on this one! You really handled that well. Someone basically attacking your customers!

She follows him off the bus. A bus stop on a quieter street.

What are you doing?

— I think you should apologise.

— Get back on the bus, you've got your seat.

— I think you should say sorry for suggesting that I'm a psycho.

— You are a psycho, you're following me now?

— Can you please apologise to me for not giving up your seat sooner?

— Fuck's sake, this is insane.

— I never swore at you, I made a reasonable request.

— Reasonable?

— A simple request and you chose to be a dick about it.

— Alright. You can obviously walk, you don't have some broken leg or some shit, do you, so why should I? You don't know. What if I had a broken leg, what if I had vertigo or like a a a brain tumour or something so my balance was all off, huh? So who's being the insensitive selfish one?

— You don't have a brain tumour.

— Yes I do.

— No you don't.

— But what if I did?

— What if I did?

— You don't.

— No, but I had sore feet and my hands hurt.

— That's not a good enough reason.

— And an imaginary brain tumour is? You just chose to be an arsehole. Admit that to yourself.

— God, leave me alone.

— Just admit to yourself that you were an arsehole, apologise to me, and then I'll leave you alone.

— Fine, I'm sorry, okay? I'm sorry. I should have given you my seat. Happy?

— More happy, yes.

— Good.

— Thanks.

— Jesus.

They both seem like they want to move but they don't.

Okay. Run along then.

— You go.

— What?

— Well, I have to wait for the next bus now. You go.

— Serious?

— I live up past the university, I'm not going to walk with all this.

— Shit.

— What?

— This isn't my stop either.

— Oh.

— I was just trying to get away from you.

They laugh a bit. Still wary.

You're a bit nuts, hey?

— You must have been so freaked out.

— Yeah I was like, really scared of you.

— I saw you there and I just snapped. Some primal thing.

— You're Croatian, right?

She nods.

Thought so.

— What about you?

— What about me what?

—

— Bit of a mix. Bosnian, I guess. From here. Not Muslim. Not practising, anyway. I'm like the worst most hard-drinking Muslim you'll ever meet.

— But your family's Muslim?

— Yep.

— And you're not?

— Yeah I just decided, hey. One day it was like, yeah, nah. I decided not to do it anymore.

— You just decided out of the blue.

— Yeah, but after you decide, you've got to follow through, hey. You gotta actually do it otherwise it's bullshit.

—

— Does that clear things up for you?

—

— Why'd you pick me, do you reckon?

—

— Yeah.

— It wasn't.

— If you say so.

— I'm I'm sorry if you thought it was, what you're suggesting it was.

— I'm not suggesting anything.

— My feet hurt.

— Okay.

—

—

— When's the bus due, do you think?

— They come every half hour. When they're on time they do, anyway, which is not very often.

— God.

— What?

— My hands are numb.

— Put your bags down.

— ?

— The ground's dry.

— Oh.

She puts the bags down. Relief. She massages her hands.

— Feel good?

— You have no idea.

— Stretch 'em out. Stretch 'em out all wide like this.

— Ahhhh.

— Feels amazing, hey.

— Yeah.

— Now make fists.

— Mmmh.

— Yeah and then out again.

— Ahh.

— Tennis.

— What?

— Used to play tennis. Then you make this like claw with your—

— Like this?

— Yeah and then—

— Ahhhhh.

— It's good, hey.

— Thanks. Yeah. They're freezing. I think. I didn't realise it was so cold.

— Yeah.

They smile at each other for a second. JANA *does the hand exercises for a while.* DINO *takes out a cigarette.*

Dino.

— Pardon.

— My name's Dino.

— Oh, Jana.

EMILY SIX	*JANA SEVEN*
After much careful deliberation and making a list of pros and cons in my notes app, I decide against walking into the sea.	
	We wait for over an hour but the bus doesn't come.
I can't give him the satisfaction of ending the story like that.	
	He asks me where I live. I tell him the suburb, not the street.
I grab the beers out of the sand and walk back towards where I parked the car.	
	He googles the distance. A twenty-five-minute walk.
Along the sand and down a little path past the surf club.	
	I know what he's suggesting but I don't bite.

I'd forgotten how silent it gets
here once the sun goes down past
the escarpment.

He says it'll rain later so unless I
feel like waiting.

I'm just being silly.

He picks up my bags and carries
them for me. We start to walk.

He's not like that.

I don't think he'll do anything.

I know he isn't.

I pull up my sister's number on
my phone.

I pull up my sister's number on
my phone.

Just in case.

Just so she's near.

I don't think he'll do anything.

He wouldn't.

But I don't know.

He's more likely to subtweet
me, I think—or scribble a thinly

veiled caricature in one of his
bullshit first-person short stories.

                    I don't know anything about him.

He'd read it out in class and
pointedly look over at me when
he uses the noun phrase 'the girl'.

                    Fuck.

Women never have names in his
stories.

                    I don't know anything about him
                    and he's walking me home.

Just Mum, Nan, her, the girl, she.

                    This is—

My car sits in the car park. It
looks

                    Wrong

Wrong somehow, it looks

                    A risk.

slumped down on its back tyres
on a weird angle. They look flat.

                    A stupid risk walking home with
                    this guy, this

Did I not notice?

Boy. This—

Did I not realise that when I
drove here?

Bosniak.

God.

God.

I start running towards the car.

Neither of us are saying anything
now.

I check the tread.

We walk like this for ages.

A ragged tear in the rubber gapes
in each of the back wheels

Ten minutes.

No.

He's standing too close.

The word PSYCHO is scratched
in sharpie on the hood.

I walk a little faster.

He's slashed my tyres.

He speeds up to match me.

He's slashed my fucking tyres.

I walk quicker.

Fuck it.

I can hear his footsteps behind me. Loud.

I break one of the beers out of the cardboard and crack it open.

Nearly at my street.

I take a long sip.

Hey, his voice behind me, gruff.

It's too much.

I start to run.

CUNT.

Wait!

CUNT.

But I don't look back just—

CUNT

Run.

I take the beer bottle and peg it, blindly. I don't care what it hits. It shatters against the wall of the surf club.

Run.

I throw another. It arcs through
the night air

Run.

hits the wall and explodes

He's still coming.

I throw the next one through the
window of the club. It's stupidly
loud.

HELP.

SMASH

SOMEONE!

OI.   OI.

He yells after me.

A voice from inside the club.
Voices.

OI.

The slapping of thongs against
bare feet. The sound of running in
thongs.

Your bags.

Flap flap flap flap flap.

My—

They'll know it was me.

Your bags, he's saying.

Men. Four men, round the corner
of the club.

OI.

I stop.

Frozen.

We're at my street.

They bolt towards me.

He catches up.

They yell out.

He's out of breath.

Did you see that?

Why'd you run off?

Someone busted the window did
ya see where he went?

What did you think was going to
happen?

I put the beer behind my back.

                              I don't know, I—

What makes you think it was
a dude? That is like a pretty
problematic attitude to—

                              Fucking hell, he says. I don't
                              know.

Did you see anyone?

                              Fucking hell, he says.

I think about how Simon's fist
clenched and unclenched.

                              And he hands me back the bags.

He was this skinny, hipster-
looking dude. He was wearing
an Adidas tracksuit and he was
heading towards the station. I
stop short of saying and his name
is Simon fucking Greenwell and
he studies Creative Writing at
USyd.

                              He took the heavy ones. The
                              olives and milk.

They thank me and run off. Their
thongs flapping against the soles
of their feet.

                              That was nice.

I feel—

                    I start to say I'm sorry but then—

Amazing.

                    But then—

I'd love to see it.

HEY   HEY.

CUNT!

                    Men. Four men, bolting towards us out of dark of the street

FUCKHEAD.

                    I know their faces. Young men from the apartment block. They reach us. What'd'you think you're doing, mate?

I hope they find him.

                    Dino steps back.

I hope they push him to the ground.

                    They shove him. Thief.

I hope they grind his face in the dirt.

No, I say. He was helping. They don't listen.

Fuck you.

Go home, they say. But he can't, because they're all around him. Pushing. He tries to break through but one puts his leg behind him and trips him backwards to the ground.

I hope he cries like a little baby.

They kick him in the face.

When they kick him.

Gypsy.

And kick him.

In the stomach. Filth.

And kick him.

In his groin. NO!

And kick him.

HE DIDN'T—

And kick him.

DIDN'T DO ANYTHING—

And kick.

PLEASE.

And

STOP!

This next section of text should be thought of as a prompt for a piece of stage action. The written text doesn't necessarily need to be spoken as long as the action of it is clear and it is the loudest bit of the play.

I drop the bags and shove one of them out of the way and throw myself on top of Dino. I lay flat. I try to spread myself out so they can't get to him. They don't stop.

In my head I'm kicking him too.

Blows land on my body but I barely feel them. It's like it's all happening to someone else.

And I'm laughing.

They try and pull me off but I cling tight. The men call me a gypsy's whore. A gob of spit lands on my cheek.

I'm laughing my head off.

They seem bored now. Over it. They throw their cigarette butts at us. The amber sparks flare out like pixels on some corrupted gif.

Did I really just do that?

> I stay lying on top of Dino for a
> long time after they leave.

I take slow deep breaths.

> We breathe in and out together.

In over six, pause for five, out
over seven.

> EMILY *breathes. She softly repeats her breathing mantra under*
> DINO *and* JANA*'s text.*
> *The text should return at this point.*

DINO: You can get off me now.

> JANA *does, slowly.* DINO *pulls himself to sitting.*

JANA. Your lip.

> DINO *gingerly touches his face and winces.*

God, your. Your—

> *She reaches to touch his face but he palms her away.*

We should get you to the hospital, we should—

> DINO *shakes his head.*
> *He drags himself to standing.*

I'm sorry, if I—Because I didn't know they'd do that.

DINO: Okay.

JANA: I don't know why I ran, I'm—

> DINO *tries to straighten his clothes up a bit, picks his phone up*
> *from the ground.* JANA *stands up.*

Let me pay for, I can pay for your your clothes or your, your phone
is it—?

DINO: It's fine.

JANA: Do you want some money?

DINO: No.

JANA: Let me give you some money.

DINO:

JANA: Or—or some of this stuff is probably—

> JANA *kneels down, crawling to pick up the groceries scattered on the ground. She holds up a can of chickpeas.*

This or—it's bit dented but you can have anything you, all of this if you want.

DINO: I'll do without.

JANA: Please?

DINO:

JANA: Please.

DINO:

JANA: Then what do I—what do I do?

DINO:

JANA: Tell me what I should do.

> DINO *looks at* JANA. *He doesn't say anything. He leaves.* JANA *starts to pick up the rest of the scattered items, putting a few things back in the bags, but then she stops. Kneeling in the wreckage of the groceries, she looks up.*

EMILY SEVEN

Mum's house is still a bombsite from the party. When she lets me in she asks have you heard from your sister? What? Isn't she here? She starts trying to tidy things up off the floor. Mum, where is she? Shh, she says, Ewen just went down. Mum! It's just that her phone's off and she didn't say when she'd be back. She probably just needed some time. No, I know, she says, she's doing the best she can and I'm happy to help it's just that I'm a bit worried that when I have to go back to work things will—she surveys the trashed house and breathes out slowly—further deteriorate. She grabs a dishcloth. Stop, Mum, I say, I'll do it. Her shoulders drop. You go to bed. It's so easy to make her happy. Why I don't do it more— She manages to refrain from outlining everything that needs to be cleaned in precise and exhausting detail. We hug goodnight. You're a good girl, she says. I'm not though.

I stack the plates, mop the tiles, retrieve the Tonka from under the lounge and bin an armful of wrapping paper. Then I wash everything up, wipe surfaces, sweep and mop. The house gleams in the blue light of the TV. Still a shithole. Just cleaner.

Then.

EMILY:	JANA:
	Baka?
Hello.	
There.	There.
It's her.	It's her.
Gemma.	Mina.
My sister.	My sister.
Back late.	Up late.
My older sister.	My younger sister.
Hi.	Hi.

EMILY AND JANA EIGHT

The living room of an apartment on Fra. Ambre Miletica, Mostar—2 a.m.

Simultaneously:

The living room of a house on Philip Street, Thirroul—2 a.m.

EMILY: Where were you?

JANA: What?

EMILY: She's been worried, she didn't know if something had happened or—

JANA: I was walking.

EMILY: Where?

JANA: Just walking. I feel like I've been everywhere.

> JANA *stumbles a little, catches herself.*

EMILY: Are you alright?

JANA: Do you ever have that thing where you're so tired you sort of feel like you're levitating?

EMILY: Sit down.

> JANA *sits. It feels incredible to sit.* EMILY *watches her.*

JANA: I thought you went out.

EMILY: I'm back.

JANA: Ah.

EMILY: Sorry about before.

JANA: That's okay?

EMILY: I'm pregnant.

> *They don't say anything for a while.* EMILY *sits.*

I think that's why everything's so horrible.

JANA:

EMILY:

JANA: What are you going to do?

EMILY: Can we not talk about it? All I've done today is talk about it.

JANA: Okay.

EMILY:

JANA: TV?

>   EMILY *nods. They look at the TV.*

EMILY: Look at him. The big man with his little glass vial of poison. And they're lighting candles. Putting out flowers.

JANA:

EMILY: What is wrong with everyone?

JANA: What do you think he's thinking? Before he takes it.

EMILY: I don't know. Fuck you, world! Remember my name! I'm a hero!

JANA: I think he just looks scared.

EMILY:

JANA: He looks really, really scared.

>   JANA *turns the TV off.*

What are you going to do?

EMILY: I'm not asking for money.

JANA: How much?

EMILY: You've got your own stuff going on, you don't need—

JANA: I want to help.

EMILY: No, I'll figure something out.

JANA: I want to.

EMILY: I should be able to do this myself.

JANA: I'll help.

EMILY: But—

JANA: What are you going to do if I don't?

EMILY:

JANA:

EMILY:

JANA: You decide what you want and I will be there.

EMILY:

JANA: No-one's going to tell you what the right thing to do is. You have to decide.

EMILY: That sucks.

JANA: Yeah, it's terrible. It's fucking horrible. The world is a terrible, horrible, fucked place.

EMILY:

JANA: I can go first if you like.

EMILY: First doing what?

JANA: Deciding what to do.

EMILY: You're just going to decide something random.

JANA: Yeah but then actually do it. You have to actually do it otherwise it's bullshit.

EMILY: What are you going to do?

JANA: Become an entirely different person.

EMILY: Fuck.

JANA: Yeah.

EMILY: Are you really?

JANA: Otherwise it's bullshit.

EMILY: Sounds hard.

JANA: Ooh yeah, that's the point.

EMILY: Okay.

JANA: Your turn.

EMILY: My turn.

JANA: Yep.

EMILY: Can I have two?

JANA: Yeah!

EMILY: Okay. One. Move back here over summer so I can pay you both back.

JANA: Oof.

EMILY: Yeah, that's the hard one.

JANA: She'd love that. You should.

EMILY: Well, I mean, I decided now so.

JANA: Okay, now the easy one.

EMILY: Number two.

JANA: Yep.

EMILY:

JANA: What?

EMILY: Save the world.

> *They look at each other.*
> *A shiver.*

JANA: Cold?

EMILY: Yeah.

JANA: Here.

> *They rug themselves up. Blankets around their shoulders.*

Big day.

EMILY: Big day.

JANA:

EMILY: Are you okay?

JANA *shakes her head.*

JANA: Are you?

EMILY *shakes her head.*
They look at each other.
They might laugh, a little, together.
The blankets over their shoulders might,
in this light,
look like capes.

THE END

GRIFFIN THEATRE COMPANY
PRESENTS

GRIFFIN
THEATRE
COMPANY

SUPERHEROES

BY MARK ROGERS

REGINALD THEATRE, SEYMOUR CENTRE
25 SEPTEMBER – 24 OCTOBER

DIRECTOR
SHARI SEBBENS

DRAMATURG
DECLAN GREENE

DESIGNER
RENÉE MULDER

LIGHTING DESIGNER
VERITY HAMPSON

**COMPOSER AND
SOUND DESIGNER**
DAVID BERGMAN

**ASSOCIATE COMPOSER
AND SOUND DESIGNER**
ALYX DENNISON

STAGE MANAGER
KHYM SCOTT

WITH
GEMMA BIRD
MATHESON
CLAIRE LOVERING
ALEKS MIKIC

With thanks to the
development cast
**Christian Byers
Brenna Harding
Nikita Waldron**

Supported by
Government partners

NSW   Australian Government   Australia
Council
for the Arts

Griffin acknowledges the generosity of the
Seaborn, Broughton & Walford Foundation in
allowing it the use of the SBW Stables Theatre
rent free, less outgoings, since 1986.

PLAYWRIGHT'S
NOTE

In late 2017, my partner Ash and I were getting ready for the arrival of our first child. I was shitting myself. I was thinking a lot about responsibility, about what it means to bring a child into the world right now. I was thinking BIG thoughts about the direction of the world, and also really practical thoughts about day care and car seats and sleep. Then in late November, I saw some footage of an ex-theatre and TV director turned General for the Bosnian-Croatian forces committing suicide during his trial for war crimes at The Hague. Somehow all of this got rolled in together to form the first draft of *Superheroes*.

It's a play about two women—Emily and Jana—one in Thirroul, NSW, and the other in Mostar, Bosnia. It asks if there is a connection between an inability to take responsibility for our actions on a personal level, and a larger failure of responsibility on an international scale. What I wanted to know was: what does it take to change your mind? What does it mean to take responsibility for your actions?

Rehearsing this play in 2020 has amplified those questions. We are faced with a crisis that demands we measure our own desires against the needs of everyone else. It demands that we take responsibility, not just for our own actions, but for the wellbeing of others as well. To do so—to really do so—we must change. The structure of our society must change. This is not a COVID play (thank f*ck!), but I hope that it somehow echoes the challenges we're dealing with today.

I also want to say something about theatre. I have missed it. I have missed its smell. Its rules and rituals. The way it makes me think. The way words bend and twist in the air of it. The stupefying power of an actor in front of an audience. The first shard of light in the dark. The stupid exit signs that spoil complete blackouts. The crackle of laughter in an audience. I've even missed the overpriced drinks. But while I'm very happy to be back, I know there are many who aren't back yet. To the freelance artists shamefully abandoned by the government's JobKeeper/JobSeeker provisions–I miss you most of all. I urge our industry, audiences and the broader community to fight for the support of these vital, vulnerable arts workers.

I'm extraordinarily stoked and grateful to heaps of people for their help with this work. To Shari, Declan and the team at Griffin for their support and faith. To Christian Byers, Brenna Harding and Nikita Waldron for their keen development brains. To my friends Hannah Goodwin, Liv Satchell and Harriet Gillies for reading early drafts of scenes and telling me to make it funnier. To Sanja Simic and Jenni Medway for shaping me as a writer and asking me hard questions. To Jelena Sajinovic for her keen insights into Mostar and the legacy of the war within the war. And, of course, to Ash Ray who is responsible for all the best bits in all my plays. Just ask her.

Thanks heaps.
Mark Rogers

DIRECTOR'S
NOTE

I first came across *Superheroes* in 2019 when it won the Patrick White Playwrights Award and was pulled into the poetry, sophistication and thrill of the piece. Profoundly generous, Mark Rogers is the type of playwright a first-time director could only dream of. Unrelenting in the interrogation of his vision, he will follow a character's thread to its deepest colour, inviting them to pull at their own snags as we, the audience, watch them unravel the world before us.

As *Superheroes* started calling into question the fragile connective tissue of community and responsibility almost two years ago, nobody knew what a flicker of hope this play would become for so many artists and creatives within the space of a few months. Blessed with a writer and dramaturg dream team, a cast of incredibly generous actors who'd not been able to open their *Kindness* season, unlimited Zoom hours and three weird and wonderful weeks of online development for what is a very offline practice; we inched ever closer to the thing we love doing most whilst never feeling further removed from it—from you. Thank you for bringing us back.

Shari Sebbens

MARK ROGERS
PLAYWRIGHT

Mark is a multi-award-winning playwright and theatremaker. Mark's theatre credits include: for Brisbane Festival: Under the Radar: *Soothsayers*; for Merrigong Theatre Company: *Tom William Mitchell*; for Novelty UK: *Target Audience*; for the Old 505 Theatre: *Plastic*; for PACT and AC Arts Adelaide: *Gobbledygook*; for Tamarama Rock Surfers and Bondi Feast: *The Buck*; for Tamarama Rock Surfers and the Old Fitzroy Theatre: *Blood Pressure* (published by PlayLab). In 2019, he won both the Griffin Award and Sydney Theatre Company's Patrick White Award for *Superheroes*, which was also shortlisted for Stuckemarkt at Theatretreffern as part of the Berlin Festspiele. Mark has produced celebrated work with some of Australia's most innovative independent companies, including Woodcourt Art Theatre, Bodysnatchers and re:group. His work on projects with the performance collective Applespiel since 2008 includes seasons at major theatres nationally and internationally. He holds a PhD from the University of Wollongong, where he works as a lecturer in theatre and performance.

SHARI SEBBENS
DIRECTOR

Shari is a Bardi, Jabirr Jabirr person born and raised on Larrakia Country, now blessed to live on Gadigal Land. Shari is the Richard Wherrett Fellow at the Sydney Theatre Company. *Superheroes* will mark her directorial debut. Shari's theatre credits as an actor include: for Griffin: *The Bleeding Tree*, *Return to Earth*; for Griffin and Queensland Theatre: *City Of Gold*; for Griffin and La Boite: *A Hoax*; for Belvoir: *Back At The Dojo*, *Radiance*; for Black Swan State Theatre Company: *Our Town*; for Darwin Festival: *Wulamanyuwi and the Seven Pamanui*; for Darwin Theatre Company: *A Midsummer Night's Dream*; for Darwin Festival and Malthouse Theatre: *Shadow King*; for Queensland Theatre: *An Octoroon*; for Sydney Theatre Company: *A Cheery Soul*, *The Battle of Waterloo*, *Black is the New White*. Shari's film credits include: *Australia Day*, *The Darkside*, *The Sapphires*, *Teenage Kicks*, *Thor: Ragnarok*, *Top End Wedding*. Her television credits include: for ABC: *8MMM Aboriginal Radio*, *Black Comedy*, *The Gods of Wheat Street*, *The Heights*, *The Letdown*, *Redfern Now* (for which she was awarded the Logie Award—Graham Kennedy Award for Most Outstanding New Talent), *Soul Mates*, *Ta Da!*; and for SBS: *A Chance Affair*. Shari trained in Aboriginal Theatre at WAAPA and graduated from NIDA with a Bachelor of Fine Arts (Acting).

DECLAN GREENE
DRAMATURG

Declan is the Artistic Director of Griffin Theatre Company, and works as a playwright, dramaturg and director. He has collaborated as a dramaturg with writers including Nakkiah Lui, Zoey Dawson, Maxine Beneba Clarke, and Future D. Fidel. As a playwright, his work includes *Eight Gigabytes of Hardcore Pornography*, *The Homosexuals, or Faggots*, *Melancholia*, *Moth*, and *Pompeii L.A.* As a director, his credits include: for Malthouse Theatre: *Wake in Fright*; for Malthouse Theatre and Sydney Theatre Company: *Blackie Blackie Brown*; for Sydney Theatre Company: *Hamlet: Prince of Skidmark*; for ZLMD Shakespeare Company: *Conviction*. He co-founded queer experimental theatre company Sisters Grimm with Ash Flanders in 2006, and has directed and co-created all their productions to date, including: for Griffin Independent and Theatre Works: *Summertime in the Garden of Eden*; for Malthouse Theatre and Sydney Theatre Company: *Calpurnia Descending*; for Melbourne Theatre Company: *Lilith: The Jungle Girl*; and for Sydney Theatre Company: *Little Mercy*. He was Resident Artist at Malthouse Theatre between 2016 and 2019.

RENÉE MULDER
DESIGNER

Renée is an award-winning set and costume designer. Her theatre design credits include: for Griffin: *The Bleeding Tree*, *The Boys*, *Prima Facie*; for Griffin Independent: *The Pigeons*; for Griffin and La Boite: *A Hoax*; for Griffin and Queensland Theatre: *Rice*; for Bell Shakespeare: *Romeo and Juliet*; for La Boite: *As You Like It*, *I Love You, Bro*, *Ruben Guthrie*; for Melbourne Theatre Company: *Arbus and West*, *Home, I'm Darling*; for Queensland Theatre: *An Octoroon*, *Fat Pig*, *Nearer the Gods*, *Sacre Bleu!*, *Triple X*; for Sydney Theatre Company: *Actor on a Box: The Luck Child*, *Banging Denmark*, *Battle of Waterloo*, *The Beauty Queen of Leenane*, *Black is the New White*, *Dance Better at Parties*, *Hamlet: Prince of Skidmark*, *In a Heart Beat*, *The Long Way Home*, *Mariage Blanc*, *Mrs Warren's Profession*, *Orlando*, *Perplex*, *The Splinter*, *The Torrents*; for Sydney Theatre Company and Queensland Theatre: *The Effect*; and for Theatre Forward: *The Sneeze*. As costume designer, her credits include: for Sydney Theatre Company: *Children of the Sun*, *Chimerica*, *Endgame*, *The Harp in the South Part One and Part Two*, *Saint Joan*, *Top Girls*; for Sydney Theatre Company and State Theatre Company of South Australia: *Vere (Faith)*. As set designer, her credits include: for Sydney Theatre Company and La Boite: *Edward Gant's Amazing Feats of Loneliness*. As associate designer, her credits include: for Sydney Theatre Company: *Cyrano de Bergerac*. Renée's film credits include, as co-production designer: *A Parachute Falling in Siberia*; as part of the armour art department: *The Chronicles of Narnia: The Voyage of the Dawn Treader*. Renée was Sydney Theatre Company's Resident Designer from 2012-2014, and was a member of Queensland Theatre's National Artistic Team from 2016-2017. She is a graduate of NIDA and Queensland College of Art.

VERITY HAMPSON
LIGHTING DESIGNER

Verity is a lighting and projection designer with over 10 years' experience, designing over 130 productions. Her theatre design credits include: for Griffin: *A Strategic Plan*, *And No More Shall We Part*, *Angela's Kitchen*, *Beached*, *The Bleeding Tree*, *The Boys*, *The Bull*, *The Moon and the Coronet of Stars*, *Dealing With Clair*, *The Floating World*, *This Year's Ashes*, *The Turquoise Elephant*; for Griffin Independent: *The Brothers Size*, *The Cold Child*, *Crestfall*, *Family Stories: Belgrade*, *Live Acts On Stage*, *Music*, *The New Electric Ballroom*, *References to Salvadore Dali Make Me Hot*, *Way to Heaven*; for Griffin and Bell Shakespeare: *The Literati*; for Bell Shakespeare: *A Midsummer Night's Dream*, *Julius Caesar*, *Titus Andronicus*; for Belvoir: *An Enemy of the People*, *The Drover's Wife*, *Faith Healer*, *Winyanboga Yurringa*; for Ensemble: *Baby Doll*, *Fully Committed*; for Malthouse Theatre: *Wake in Fright*; for Queensland Theatre: *Death of a Salesman*; and for Sydney Theatre Company: *Blackie Blackie Brown*, *Hamlet: Prince of Skidmark*, *Machinal*, *Little Mercy*. Verity has won two Sydney Theatre Awards and a Green Room Award for Best Mainstage Lighting Design, as well as an APDG Award for Best Lighting Design. She is a NIDA graduate.

DAVID BERGMAN
COMPOSER AND SOUND DESIGNER

David is a composer, sound and video designer and has been based in Sydney for over 10 years. His recent work includes: as Composer and Sound Designer: for Griffin: *First Love is the Revolution*; for Darlinghurst Theatre Company: *Maggie Stone*; for NIDA: *Another Country*, *SALEM*; for Seymour Centre: *Made to Measure*; as Sound and Video Designer: for Sydney Theatre Company: *A Cheery Soul*, *The Wharf Revue* (2009-2019); for Soft Tread Enterprises: *The Gospel According to Paul*; as Sound Designer: for ATYP: *Spring Awakening*; for Hayes Theatre Company: *Catch Me If You Can*, *The Rise and Disguise of Elizabeth R*; for Monkey Baa: *Josephine Wants to Dance*; as Co-Sound Designer: for Belvoir: *Packer and Sons*; and as Video Designer: for Bangarra: *Knowledge Ground*; for Monkey Baa: *The Peasant Prince*, *Possum Magic*; for Sydney Chamber Opera: *Breaking Glass*; for Sydney Theatre Company: *The Effect*, *The Hanging*, *The Long Way Home*, *Muriel's Wedding the Musical*. David was the Technical Director for *Griffin Lock-In* in 2020. David trained at NIDA and teaches for their graduate and postgraduate courses.

ALYX DENNISON
ASSOCIATE COMPOSER AND SOUND DESIGNER

Alyx Dennison is a Sydney-based singer, composer and sound artist. She was one half of the critically acclaimed duo *kyü* alongside Freya Berkhout, and played festivals including The Great Escape (UK), Homebake, Meredith Musical Festival, Mona Foma Festival, and SXSW (US) before releasing their first studio album in 2010 through Popfrenzy/Inertia. In 2011, they were awarded the Qantas Spirit of Youth Award and disbanded on a high with the release of their second album in 2012. In 2015, Alyx released her solo debut album with Popfrenzy/Caroline, which she toured nationally, as well as supporting Deradoorian (Dirty Projectors), Juana Molina (Argentina) and LAMB (UK). As lead vocalist and instrumentalist, Alyx's performance credits include: for the Biennale of Sydney: *Composition for Mouths*; for Big hART: *SKATE*; for Liveworks: *Day for Night* (alongside Nick Wales, Ngaiire, Stereogamous and the Inner West Voices), *Invisible, As Music, The Other Tempo, Rhetorical Chorus*; for MUMA and Google: *Wet Matter*; for Sydney Contemporary: *Bravi Brava Brave*; for Shaun Parker Company: *Am I* (Tour). As Composer and Sound Designer, Alyx's credits include: for Griffin: *Splinter*; for All About Women Festival/Giant Dwarf: *Story Club Solo: Zoe Norton Lodge*; for Dance Massive: *CO_EX_EN*; for Dirty Feet/Dance Bites: *Double Beat*; for MUMA: *The Door*; for Next Wave Festival: *mi:wi*; for Transit Dance Company: *ID;* as well as work on a new feature dance work and short film with Cass Eipper and the Australasian Dance Collective. As Record Producer, credits include: for Bonniesongs: *Energetic Mind* (Smallpond UK); for Pheno: *Dragon Year* (Electric Ear Records); as well as current work on an album with Jessica O'Donoghue. Alyx is also a music educator, and has worked as a mentor for Campbelltown Arts Centre/Bree van Reyks's *Massive Band*; at Liverpool Girls' High School; and for *Wandering Books*, a music outreach program for refugee students in primary schools across Western Sydney. Alyx is currently developing her second solo release with the support of Campbelltown Arts Centre. She studied composition at VCA.

KHYM SCOTT
STAGE MANAGER

Khym has previously worked for Griffin Theatre Company as Stage Manager: *Family Values, First Love is the Revolution, City of Gold, Prima Facie, Good Cook. Friendly. Clean., Kill Climate Deniers, Festival of New Writing, The Witches, Girl in Tan Boots, The Serpent's Table*; as Broadcast Director: *Griffin Lock-In; Griffin Award 2020*; and for Griffin/Bell Shakespeare: *The Misanthrope*. Other recent credits include: for Belvoir/Malthouse: *Barbara and the Camp Dogs*; for Belvoir: *The Dance of Death, Miss Julie, This Heaven*; for Contemporary Asian Australian Performance: *Double Delicious, Stories Then and Now*; for Sydney Festival: *Lady Rizo: Red, White and Indigo*; and for the Sydney Gay and Lesbian Mardi Gras. From 2013 to 2017, Khym was Assistant Stage Manager of The Australian Ballet, and toured with the company regionally, nationally, and internationally. Khym is a graduate of NIDA and The University of Sydney.

GEMMA BIRD MATHESON
EMILY

Gemma was one of the 10 finalists for the 2018 Heath Ledger Scholarship and is both an actor and writer/creator. Gemma's theatre credits include: for She Said Theatre: *Fallen*; for Sydney Theatre Company: *Orange Thrower* (Rough Draft); for VCA: *Zone Four*. Gemma's film credits include: *The Drownsman*. Gemma's television credits include: for ABC: *Bertram Poppingstock: Problem Solver*, *Content*, *Trip for Biscuits*, *Why Are You Like This*?; for Channel Seven: *Winners & Losers*; for Fremantle Media and Channel Eleven: *Neighbours*; for the SyFy Channel: *Childhood's End*. Gemma's web series credits include: as co-creator, co-writer, executive producer and performer: for ABC: *The Housemate*; as performer: *Deadhouse Dark*, *Double Date Night*. Gemma has trained at the Atlantic Theatre Company in New York, Armstrong Acting Studios in Toronto and NIDA's Young Actors Studio.

CLAIRE LOVERING
JANA

Claire graduated from WAAPA in 2010 and was awarded the Leslie Anderson Award and the Sally Burton Award that same year. Her theatre credits include: for Griffin: *The Feather in the Web*; for ATYP: *Mr Kolpert*; for Black Swan State Theatre Company: *The Damned Water Rising*, *Day One, A Hotel, Evening*; for Darlinghurst Theatre Company: *Detroit*; for Ensemble Theatre: *Who's Afraid of Virginia Woolf?*; for Kay & McLean Productions: *The Graduate*; for the Old 505 Theatre: *River*; for Sport for Jove: *The Importance of Being Earnest*; for Sydney Theatre Company: *Dinner*, *Top Girls*; for Queensland Theatre and Black Swan State Theatre Company: *Managing Carmen*; for WAAPA: *Arabian Nights*, *The Comedy of Errors*, *Joking Apart*, *The Threepenny Opera*, *Under Milk Wood*. Claire's film credits include: *San Andreas*, *Event Zero*. Her television credits include: for ABC/Netflix: *The Letdown*; for Nine Network: *Hyde & Seek*, *Bite Club*; for Network Ten: *Wonderland*. Claire's debut self-penned solo show *RIVER* won the Adelaide Fringe Weekly Award for Best Theatre and Sydney's Spectrum Now ANZ Blue Rooms Series for most promising emerging theatre talent. As a recipient of a 2015 Major Mike Walsh Fellowship, Claire travelled to New York to study method acting at the Lee Strasberg Theatre and Film Institute in 2016.

ALEKS MIKIC
SIMON / DINO

Aleks is a WAAPA Acting graduate and co-founder of artist-run-initiative and gallery Flow Studios. His theatre credits include: for Red Line Productions at the Old Fitz: *Are We Awake?;* for Sydney Opera House: *Ghost Stories;* for Sydney Theatre Company: *Dinner;* for Zen Zen Zo: *Amadeus, The Tempest.* Aleks's film credits include: *Better Watch Out, Joe Cinque's Consolation, On It Goes.* Aleks's television credits include: for ABC: *100% Wolf, Diary of an Uber Driver;* for AMC: *Preacher;* for Channel 10: *Five Bedrooms;* for Foxtel: *Secret City.* Aleks is an artist of Serbian ancestry working as a filmmaker and musician on land rightfully belonging to the Gadigal people of the Eora Nation. Aleks acknowledges with utmost respect the Indigenous Australian people as the lawful owners and custodians of this stolen land.

ABOUT GRIFFIN

Griffin is the only theatre company in the country entirely devoted to producing new Australian plays. Located in the historic SBW Stables Theatre, nestled in the heart of bustling Kings Cross, Griffin has been a permanent home for the exploration of Australian stories since 1978.

Many of this country's most beloved and celebrated artists started out on our stage—Cate Blanchett, Michael Gow, Louis Nowra, David Wenham, to name a few—and iconic Australian plays like *The Boys*, *Holding the Man* and *The Bleeding Tree* had their world premieres at Griffin, before going on to capture the national imagination. We are a theatre of first chances.

We are passionate about nurturing emerging artists. We help ambitious, bold, risk-taking and urgent Australian plays get from a page onto a stage. We tell the stories that will help us know who we are as a nation, and who we want to become.

Stories about us. Written by us. For us.

At Griffin Theatre Company, we acknowledge that our home — the SBW Stables Theatre—is built on the unceded land of the Gadigal People of the Eora Nation. It is a privilege to perform on this land, which has been a place of story, song, and community for tens of thousands of years. We offer deep and humble respect to Gadigal elders, past and present. This always was, always will be Aboriginal land.

GRIFFIN THEATRE COMPANY
13 Craigend St
Kings Cross NSW 2011
02 9332 1052
info@griffintheatre.com.au
griffintheatre.com.au

SBW STABLES THEATRE
10 Nimrod St
Kings Cross NSW 2011

BOOKINGS
griffintheatre.com.au
02 9361 3817

GRIFFIN FAMILY

GRIFFIN DONORS

Income from Griffin activities covers less than 40% of our operating costs—leaving an ever increasing gap for us to fill through government funding, sponsorship and the generosity of our individual supporters. Your support helps us bridge the gap and keep ticket prices affordable and our work at its best. To make a donation and a difference, contact Griffin on **9332 1052** or donate online at **griffintheatre.com.au**

COMPANY PATRONS
Merilyn Sleigh
& Raoul de Ferranti

PRODUCTION PATRON
Girgensohn Foundation

PROGRAM PATRONS
Season Partner
The Neilson Foundation

Griffin Ambassadors
Robertson Foundation

Griffin Studio
Gil Appleton
Darin Cooper Foundation
Kiong Lee & Richard Funston
Rosemary Hannah & Lynette Preston
Ken & Lilian Horler
Pip Rath & Wayne Lonergan
Malcolm Robertson Foundation
Geoff & Wendy Simpson
Danielle Smith
Walking up the Hill Foundation

Griffin Women's Initiative
Griffin Women's Initiative is supported by Creative Partnerships Australia through Plus1

Katrina Barter
Wendy Blacklock
Christy Boyce &
Madeleine Beaumont
Laura Crennan
Lyndell Droga
Melinda Graham
Sherry Gregory
Antonia Haralambis
Ann Johnson
Roanne Knox
Julia Pincus
Ruth Ritchie
Lenore Robertson

Sonia Simich
Margie Sullivan
Simone Whetton

SEASON PATRONS
As a new writing theatre, we program a wide range of stories that reflect our time, place and the unique voice of contemporary Australia. To ensure that these stories continue to be told, Griffin needs the help of private support to bring strength, insight, candour and new and powerful visions to the stage. Our Production Partner program is vital to our continued artistic success.

Kindness by Matthew Whittet
Darin Cooper Foundation

Prima Facie by Suzie Miller
Robert Dick & Erin Shiel
Richard McHugh
& Kate Morgan
Andrew Post & Sue Quill
Richard Weinstein
& Richard Benedict

City of Gold by Meyne Wyatt
Andrew Cameron AM & Cathy Cameron
Bruce Meagher & Greg Waters
Julia Pincus & Ian Learmonth
Malcolm Robertson Foundation
David Marr &
Sebastian Tesoriero
The Sky Foundation
Kim Williams AM &
Catherine Dovey
Ann & Brian O'Connell (in memoriam)

Splinter by Hilary Bell
Stephen Fitzgerald

SEASON DONORS
Front Row Donors +$10,000
Mary Ann Rolfe
Andrew Cameron AM &
Cathy Cameron
Darin Cooper Foundation
Robert Dick & Erin Shiel
Gordon & Marie Esden
Stephen Fitzgerald
The Girgensohn Foundation
Rosemary Hannah &
Lynette Preston
Belinda Hazelton &
Vicki Archer
Ingrid Kaiser
Malcolm Robertson Foundation
Sophie McCarthy &
Antony Green
Richard McHugh &
Kate Morgan
Bruce Meagher & Greg Waters
Peter & Dianne O'Connell
Rebel Penfold-Russell OAM
Julia Pincus & Ian Learmonth
Pip Rath & Wayne Lonergan
Robertson Foundation
Mary Ann Rolfe
The Neilson Foundation
The Sky Foundation
Merilyn Sleigh &
Raoul de Ferranti
Kim Williams AM &
Catherine Dovey

Main Stage Donor
$5,000 - $9,999
Anonymous (1)
Antoniette Albert
Gil Appleton
Lisa Barker & Don Russell
Wendy Blacklock
Ellen Borda
Louise Christie
Bernard Coles

GRIFFIN DONORS

Lyndell & Daniel Droga
Danny Gilbert AM &
Kathleen Gilbert
Ken & Lilian Horler
Kiong Lee & Richard Funston
Lee Lewis & Brett Boardman
David Marr &
Sebastian Tesoriero
Catriona Morgan-Hunn
Don & Leslie Parsonage
Anthony Paull
Sue Procter
Geoff & Wendy Simpson
Danielle Smith & Sean Carmody
Walking Up the Hill Foundation

Final Draft $2,000-$4,999
Gae Anderson
Baly Douglass Foundation
Helen Bauer & Helen Lynch AM
Marilyn & David Boyer
Iolanda Capodanno
Alan Colletti
Bryony & Tim Cox
Lachlan Edwards
Elizabeth Fullerton
Kathy Glass
Jocelyn Goyen
GRANTPIRRIE/privare
Libby Higgin
Roanne & John Knox
Carina G. Martin
Janet Manuell
John McCallum & Jenny
Nicholls
John Mitchell
David Nguyen
Chris Reed
Leslie Stern
Stuart Thomas
Tea Uglow
Richard Weinstein & Richard
Benedict

**Workshop Donor
$1,000-$1,999**
Anonymous (4)
Michael Barnes
Katrina Barter
Cheery & Peter Best

Andrew Bell & Joanna Bird
Christy Boyce & Madeleine
Beaumont
Keith Bradley AM
Michael & Charmaine Bradley
Dr Bernadette Brennan
Jane Bridge
Corinne & Bryan
Stephen & Annabelle Burley
Susan Carleton
Adrian Christie
Sally Crawford
Laura Crennan
Nathan Croft & James White
Cris Croker & David West
Jane Curry
Timothy Davis
Carol Dettman
T Dolland & S McComb
Sue and Jim Dominguez
Christine Dunstan
Bob Ernst
Ros & Paul Espie
Brian Everingham
John & Libby Fairfax
Rowena Falzon
Robyn Fortescue & Rosie
Wagstaff
Jennifer Giles
Nicky Gluyas
Melinda Graham
Peter Gray & Helen Thwaites
Reg Graycar
Sherry Gregory
Antonia Haralambis
Judge Joe Harman
Kate Harrison
James Hartwright &
Kerrin D'Arcy
Johh Head
Danielle Hoareau
Mark Hopkinson &
Michelle Opie
Susan Hyde
Ann Johnson
Margaret Johnston
Deborah Jones
David & Adrienne Kitching
Jennifer Ledgar & Bob Lim

Richard & Elizabeth Longes
Chris Marrable & Kate
Richardson
Jane Munro
Elaine & Bill McLaughlin
Dr Steve McNamara
Kent and Sandra McPhee
Joy Minter
Kate Mulvany
Tommy Murphy
John Nerthercoate
Ian Neuss & Penny Young
Patricia Novikoff
Ian Phipps
Martin Portus
Steve & Belinda Rankine
Sylvia Rosenblum
David & Dianne Russell
Sonia Simich
Jann Skinner
Geoffrey Starr
Robyn Stone
Adam Suckling &
Pip McGuinness
Margie Sullivan
Peter Talbot
Mike Thompson
Sue Thomson
Daniel P. Tobin
Janet Wahlquist
Simone Whetton
Rosemary White
Paul & Jennifer Winch
Elizabeth Wing
Kathy Zeleny

Reading Donor $500-$999
Anonymous (3)
Brian Abel
Amity Alexander
Jes Andersen
Robyn Ayres
Melissa Ball
Nikki Barrett
Penny Beran
Cherry & Peter Best
Phillip Black
Anne Britton
Annie Bourke
Larry Boyd & Barbara Caine AM

GRIFFIN DONORS

Simon Burke AO
Marianne Bush
Bill Calcraft
Gaby Carney
Jane Christensen
Amanda Clark
Eloise Curry
Melita Daru
David Davies
Michael Diamond
Max Dingle
Tim Duggan
David Earp
Wendy Elder
Leonie Flannery
Peter Graves
Tonkin Zulaikha Greer
Edwina Guinness
Stephanie & Andrew Harrison
Mary Holt
David Hoskins & Paul McKnight
Sylvia Hrovatin
Marian & Nabeel Ibrahim
Mira Joksovic
David Jonas
Susan J Kath
Susan Kippax
Maruschka Loupis
Anne Loveridge
Ian & Elizabeth MacDonald
Robert Marks
Rebecca Massey
Christopher McCabe
Wendy McCarthy AO
Patrick McIntyre
Nicole McKenna
Paula McLean
Keith Miller
Stephen Mills
Neville Mitchell
Sarah Mort
William Peck
Carolyn Penfold
Judy Phillips
Malcolm Poole
Chris Puplick
David Purves
Jennifer Rani
Alex-Oonagh Redmond

Annabel Ritchie
Jonquil Ritter
Roslyn Renwick
Judith & Frank Robertson
Colleen Roche
Karen Rodgers & Bill Harris
Gemma Rygate
Rob & Rae Spence
Mary Stollery & Eric Dole
Catherine Sullivan &
Alexandra Bowen
Pearl Tan & Priya Roy
Ariadne Vromen
Jonathan Ware
John Waters
Rosemary White
William Zappa

First Draft Donor $200–$499
Anonymous (8)
Nicole Abadee & Rob Macfarlan
Susan Ambler
Elizabeth Antonievich
Barbara Armitage
William Armitage
Wendy Ashton
Chris Baker
Jan Barr
Edwina Birch
Rebecca Bourne Jones
Elizabeth Boyd
Shay Bristowe
Peter Brown
Dean Bryant & Mathew Frank
Wendy Buswell
Ruth Campbell
David Caulfield
Charlie Chan & Angela Catterns
Peter Chapman
Sue Clark
Amanda Connelly
Brendan Crotty & Darryl Toohey
Bryan Cutler
Owen Davies
Dora Den Hengst
Joanne & Sue Dalton
Susan Donnelly
Dr June Donsworth
Peter Duerden

Anna Duggan
Michele Dulcken
Kathy Esson
Elizabeth Evatt
Michael Eyers
Eamon Flack
Paul Fletcher
Helen Ford
Lee French
Matt Garrett
Sarah & Braith Gilchrist
Jock Given
Deane Golding
Thomas Gottlieb
Brenda Gottsche
Keith Gow
Hannah Grant
Virginia & Kieran Greene
Jo Grisard
Sue Hackett
Jennifer Hagan & Ron Blair
Glen Hamilton
Elizabeth Hanley
Carol Hargreaves
Raewyn Harlock
Grania Hickley
Stephanie Hui
Matthew Huxtable
C John Keightley
Maria Kelly
James Kelly & Beu Phuong
Catherine Kennedy
Penelope Latey
Peta Leemen
Karen Lee Smith
Antoinette Le Marchant
Caleb Lewis
Mark Lillis
Liz Locke
Norman Long
Dr Peter Louw
Carolyn Lowry
Anni Macdougall
Guillermo Martin
Katrina Matthews
Louise McDonald
Edward McGuiness
Duncan McKay
Ellen McLoughlin

GRIFFIN DONORS

Ian McMillan
Sarah Miller
Bruce Milthorpe
Julia Mitchell
Catherine Moore
Pam Morris
Mullinars Casting Consultants
Dian Neligan
Carolyn Newman
Gennie Nevinson &
Vivian Manwaring
Anthony Ong
Sally Patten
Susheela Peres Da Costa
Peter Pezzutti
Meredith Phelps
Belinda Piggott &
David Ojerholm
Marion Potts
Christopher Powell
Janelle Prescott
Andrew Pringle
Virginia Pursell
Steve Riethoff
Thelma Roach
In memory of Katherine
Robertson
Ann Rocca
·Catherine Rothery
Kevin and Shirley Ryan
Sharryn Ryan
Emily Scanlan
Julianne Schultz

Julia Selby
Diana Simmonds
Bridget Smith
Vanda & Martin Smith
Camilla Strang
The Steiner Family
Augusta Supple
Margot Tanjutco
Mark & Susan Tennant
Jane Theau
Elizabeth Thompson
Stephen Thompson
Susan Tiffin
Lawrence Vaux
Richard Vickery
Christophe Vivien
Belinda Wallington
Erik van Werven
Deanna Weir
Jennifer White
Ruth Wilson
Margaret Winn
Greg Wood
Eve Wynhausen
Robert Yuen
Aviva Ziegler

*We would also like to thank
Peter O'Connell for his expertise,
guidance and time.*

Current as of 23 July 2020

SPONSORS

Government Supporters

Australian Government | Australia Council for the Arts

NSW GOVERNMENT

Patron 2020 Season

Production Partner

GIRGENSOHN FOUNDATION

2020 Season Sponsor

alphabet.

Griffin Award

COPYRIGHT AGENCY CULTURAL FUND

Griffin Studio

MALCOLM ROBERTSON FOUNDATION

Griffin Ambassadors & Artistic Associate Sponsor

ROBERTSON FOUNDATION

Creative Partners

Brett Boardman Photography

PLAYKING FOUNDATION

Company Lawyers

MARQUE

Company Sponsors

SATURDAY PAPER

THE UNIVERSITY OF SYDNEY PERFORMANCE STUDIES

Rosenfeld, Kant & Co. Business & Financial Solutions

bourke street bakery

CURRENCY PRESS

Coopers

FOUR PILLARS SMALL AUSTRALIAN DISTILLERY

MOPPITY

TimeOut

Access Partner

DESIGNKING COMPANY

Griffin Theatre Company is assisted by the Australian Government through the Australia Council, its arts funding and advisory body; and the NSW Government through Create NSW.

www.ingramcontent.com/pod-product-compliance
Lightning Source LLC
Chambersburg PA
CBHW050021090426

42734CB00021B/3367